Cantonese for Kids: A Cantonese-English Book

MY FIRST ANIMALS IN CANTONESE
動物-粵英語對照

BY KAREN YEE

FOR MOM & DAD

For a free audio recording and other books visit:
www.greencowsbooks.com

(c) 2017, Karen Yee.
Published by Green Cows Books
Inquiries: greencowsbooks@gmail.com

All rights reserved. No portion of this book may be reproduced in any form without the prior written permission of the author.

The scanning, uploading and distribution of this book via the Internet or by any other means without the express written permission of the author is illegal and punishable by law. Please purchase only authorized printed or electronic editions and do not participate in or encourage piracy of copyrighted materials. The author appreciates your support of author's rights.

ISBN: 978-0-9992730-0-5 (paperback); 978-1-955188-08-1 (hardback)

PICTURE CREDITS
Harp Seal: By Matthieu Godbout (Own work) [GFDL (http://www.gnu.org/copyleft/fdl.html), CC-BY-SA-3.0 (http://creativecommons.org/licenses/by-sa/3.0/) or CC BY-SA 2.5-2.0-1.0 (http://creativecommons.org/licenses/by-sa/2.5-2.0-1.0)], via Wikimedia Commons;
Zoo: By Czech Wikipedia user Packa (Own work) [CC BY-SA 3.0 (http://creativecommons.org/licenses/by-sa/3.0)], via Wikimedia Commons; Porcupine: By tontantravel [CC BY-SA 2.0 (http://creativecommons.org/licenses/by-sa/2.0)], via Wikimedia Commons;
Hammerhead Shark: By Barry Peters (Flickr) [CC BY 2.0 (http://creativecommons.org/licenses/by/2.0)], via Wikimedia Commons;
Gorilla: flickr.com: https://creativecommons.org/licenses/by-sa/2.0/ - Philip Kromer
Cover: Maltese (maxpixel.net; CC0), Clown Fish and Cat (Pixabay), Red Panda (Pexels)

我哋去...
ngo5 dei6 heoi3 ...
(ngo day heoi ...)
We're going to the ...

農場
nung4 coeng4
(nuong cherng)

farm

動物園
dung6 mat6 jyun4
(duong mutt yuen)

zoo

公園
gung1 jyun2
(guong yuen)

park

海邊
hoi2 bin1
(hoy bean)

oceanside

去到!
heoi3 dou3!
(heoi doh!)

We're there!

農場
nung4 coeng4
(nuong cherng)

farm

(literally: Went!)

你見唔見到隻...?
nei5 gin3 m4 gin3 dou2 zek3 ...?
(nay geen m geen doh jaek...?)

Do you see the ...?

貓
maau1
(mao)

cat

狗
gau2
(guw)

dog

(literally: Do you see or not see the ___?)

我見到隻...
ngo5 gin3 dou2 zek3 ...
(ngo geen doh jaek ...)

I see a ...

火雞
fo2 gai1
(fuoh gai)

turkey

豬
zyu1
(juu)

pig

雞
gai1
(gai)

chicken

牛
ngau4
(nguw)
cow

山羊
saan1 joeng4
(sahn yerng)
goat

馬
maa5
(mah)
horse

綿羊
min4 joeng2
(meen yerng)
sheep

咁好玩!
gam3 hou2 waan2!
(gum ho wahn!)
So much fun!

動物園
dung6 mat6 jyun4
(duong mutt yuen)

ZOO

隻 ... 好大.
zek3 ... hou2 daai6.
(jaek ... ho dye.)

The ... is very big.

河馬
ho4 maa5
(huoh mah)

hippo

大笨象
daai6 ban6 zoeng6
(dye bun jerng)

elephant

... 爬樹!
... paa4 syu6!
(... pah shue!)

... is climbing the tree!

大猩猩
daai6 sing1 sing1
(dye sing sing)
gorilla

馬騮
maa5 lau1
(mah luw)

monkey

花豹
faa1 paau3
(fah pau)

leopard

長頸鹿
coeng4 geng2 luk2
(cherng gang luuhk)

真係高!
zan1 hai6 gou1!
(jun high goh!)

So very tall!

鴕鳥
to4 niu5
(tuoh niew)

giraffe

ostrich

好多動物!
hou2 do1 dung6 mat6!
(ho duoh duong mutt!)

Lots of animals!

火烈鳥
fo2 lit6 niu5
(fuoh leet niew)

flamingo

獵豹
lip6 paau3
(leep pau)

cheetah

鱷魚
ngok6 jyu4
(nguok yue)

crocodile

狼
long4
(luong)

wolf

我鍾意隻…
ngo5 zung1 ji3 zek3 …
(ngo joe(ng) yee jaek …)

I like the …

熊
hung4
(hoe(ng))

bear

狐狸
wu4 lei2
(woo lay)

fox

老虎
lou5 fu2
(loh foo)
tiger

小熊貓
siu2 hung4 maau1
(siew hoe(ng) mao)
red panda

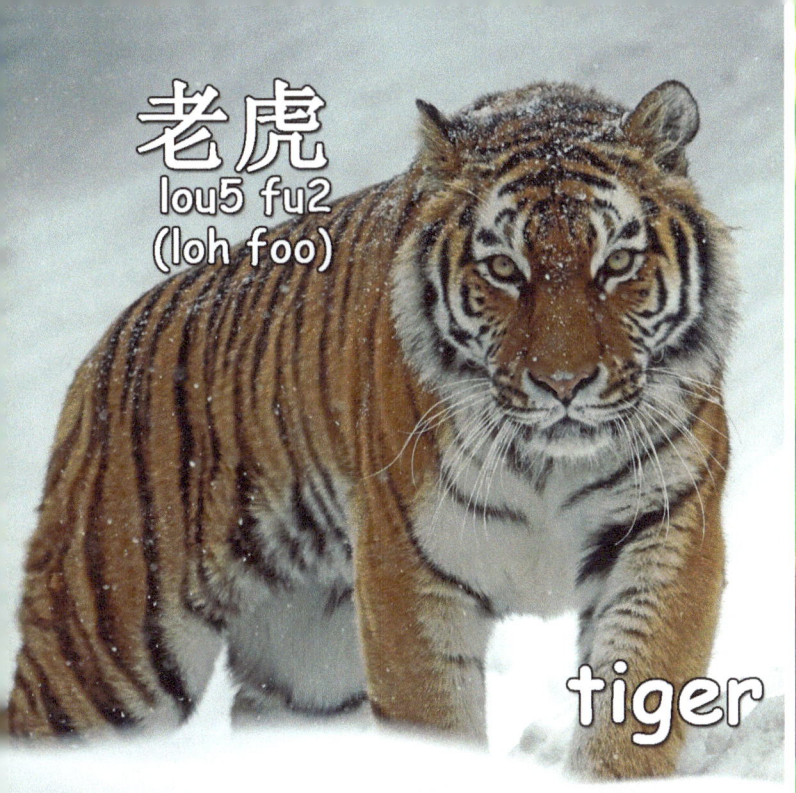

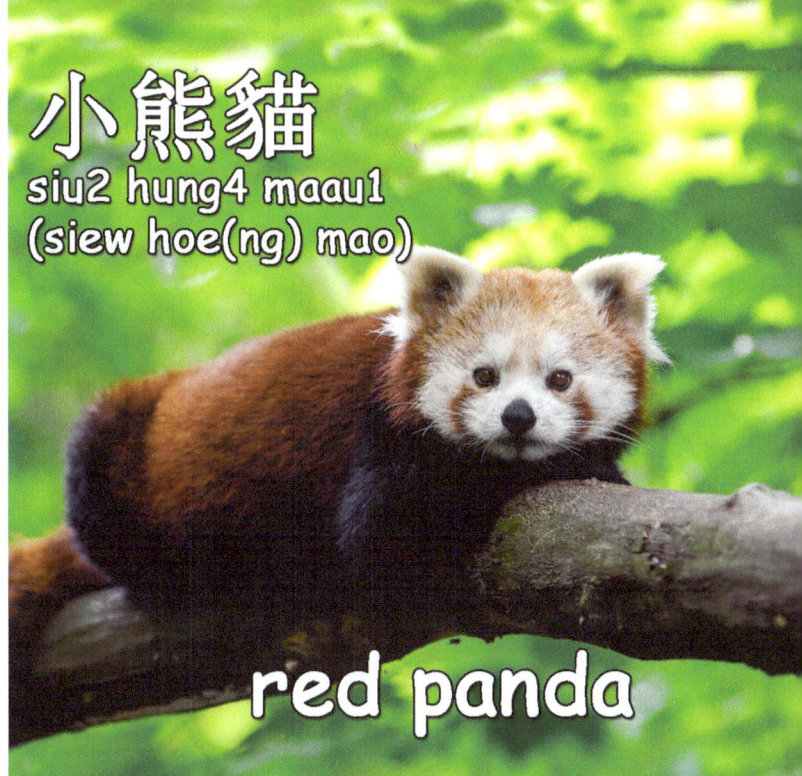

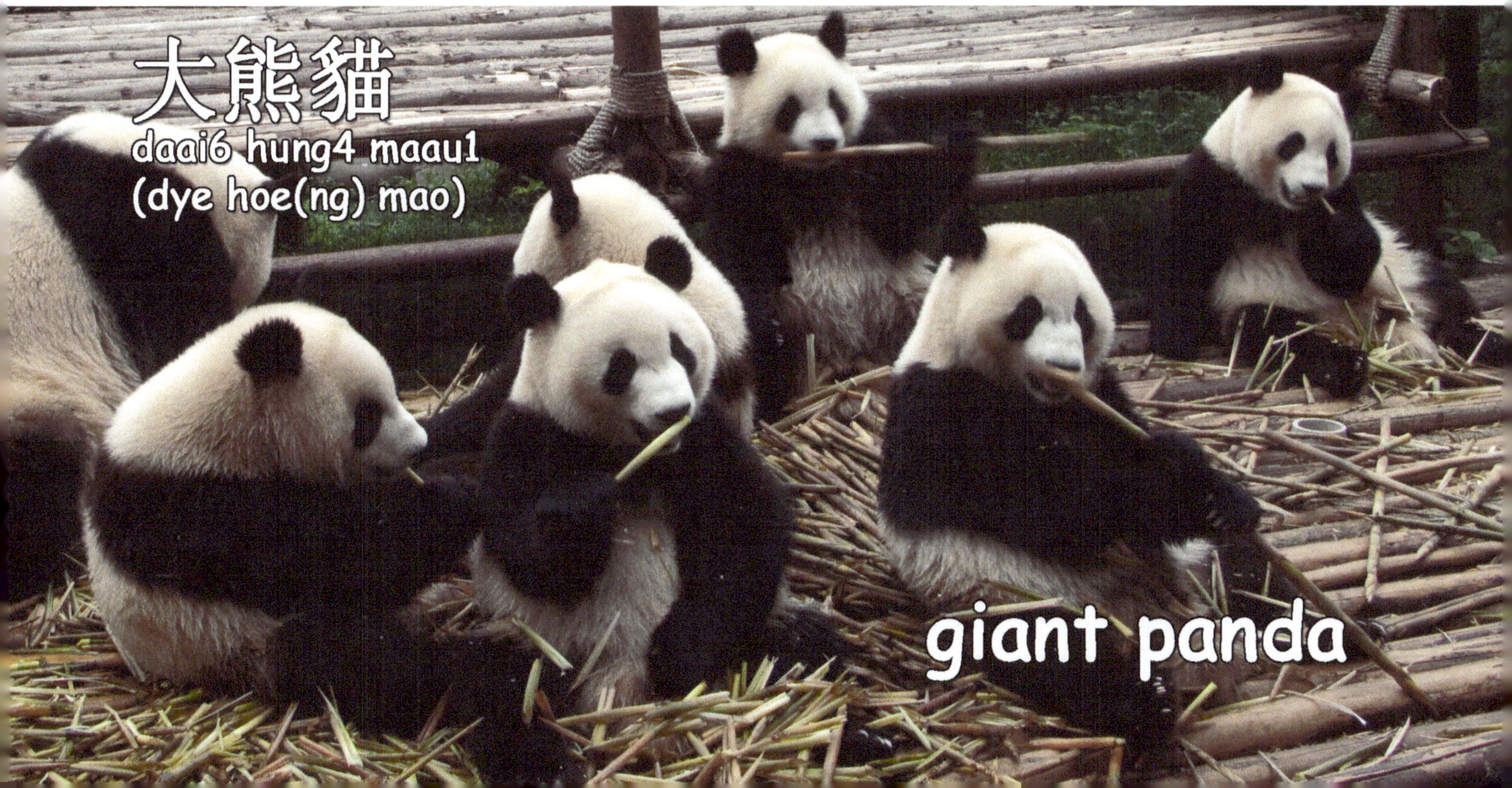
大熊貓
daai6 hung4 maau1
(dye hoe(ng) mao)
giant panda

你想睇乜野?
nei5 soeng2 tai2 mat1 je5?
(nay serng tai mutt yeh?)

What do you want to see?

袋鼠
doi6 syu2
(doy shue)

kangaroo

樹熊
syu6 hung4
(shue hoe(ng))

koala

鸚鵡
jing1 mou5
(ying moh)

parrot

我想睇...
ngo soeng2 tai2 ...
(ngo serng tai ...)

I want to see a ...

孔雀
hung2 zoek3
(hoe(ng) jerk)

peacock

駱駝
lok3 to4
(luok tuoh)

camel

佢好得意!
keoi5 hou2 dak1 ji3!
(koei ho duk yee!)

It's very cute!

企鵝
kei5 ngo2
(kay ngoh)

penguin

北極熊
bak1 gik6 hung4
(buk gik hoe(ng))

polar bear

海狗
hoi2 gau2
(hoy guw)

seal

去邊度?
heoi3 bin1 dou6?
(heoi bean doh?)

Where to?

公園
gung1 jyun2
(guong yuen)

park

(literally: Going where?)

鴨
aap3
(ahp)
duck

你最鍾意乜野?
nei5 zeoi3 zung1 ji3 mat1 je5?
(nay jui joe(ng) yee mutt yeh?)

What do you like most?

天鵝
tin1 ngo4
(teen ngo)
swan

鵝
ngo4
(ngo)
goose

我最鍾意...
ngo5 zeoi3 zung1 ji3 ...
(ngo jui joe(ng) yee ...)

I most like ...

兔仔
tou3 zai2
(toe zhai)

rabbit

松鼠
cung4 syu2
(choe(ng) shue)

squirrel

鹿
luk6
(luuhk)

deer

嗰隻係乜野?
go2 zek3 hai6 mat1 je5?
(guoh jaek hai mutt yeh?)

What is that?

鹽蛇
jim4 se2
(yeem saeh)

lizard

青蛙
cing1 waa1
(ching wah)

frog

臭鼠
cau3 syu2
(chuw shue)

skunk

嗰隻係...
go2 zek3 hai6...
(guoh jaek hai...)

That's a ...

貓頭鷹
maau1 tau4 jing1
(mao tuw ying)

owl

老鼠
lou5 syu2
(loh shue)

mouse

浣熊
wun5 hung4
(wuun hoe(ng))

raccoon

到啦!
dou3 laa1!
(doh lah!)
We're there!

海邊
hoi2 bin1
(hoy bean)

oceanside

(literally: Arrived!)

條... 跳!
tiu4 ... tiu3!
(tiew ... tiew!)

The ... jumps!

鯨魚
king4 jyu2
(king yue)
whale

殺人鯨
saat3 jan4 king4
(saht yen king)
killer whale

... 游水!
... jau4 seoi2!
(... yuw seoi!)

The ... is swimming!

鯊魚
saa1 jyu4
(sah yue)

shark

海豚
hoi2 tyun4
(hoy toone)

dolphin

錘頭鯊魚
ceoi4 tau4 saa1 jyu4
(cheoi tuw sah yue)

hammerhead shark

魷魚
jau4 jyu2
(yuw yue)

squid

魔鬼魚
mo1 gwai2 jyu2
(muoh gwie yue)

stingray

墨魚
mak6 jyu4
(muk yue)

cuttlefish

好靚!
hou2 leng3!
(ho lang!)

Very pretty!

海星
hoi2 sing1
(hoy sing)

seastar

蝦
haa1
(ha)

shrimp

八爪魚
baat3 zaau2 jyu4
(baht jau yue)

octopus

海馬
hoi2 maa5
(hoy mah)

seahorse

白鮓
baak6 zaa3
(bahk jah)

jellyfish

魚
jyu2
(yue)

fish

貝殼
bui3 hok3
(boui huok)

seashell

睇佢行!
tai2 keoi5 haang4!
(tai koei hahng!)

Look at it walk!

海獅
hoi2 si1
(hoy see)

sea lion

海龜
hoi2 gwai1
(hoy gwigh)

sea turtle

蟹
haai5
(high)

crab

返屋企!
faan1 uk1 kei2!
(fahn uhk kay!)
Going home!

屋企
uk1 kei2
(uhk kay)

home

NOTES

REMEMBERING CANTONESE TONES

Each Jyutping includes the tone (example: 貓 maau1 = tone 1). The six tones can be remembered using a mnemonic. To remember the Cantonese tones in order, speak the numbers "394052"(saam1 gau2 sei3 ling4 ng5 ji6) in Cantonese.

TONE	NUMBER	JYUTPING	ALTERNATE PHONETICS
Tone 1	"3"	saam1	sahm
Tone 2	"9"	gau2	guw
Tone 3	"4"	sei3	say
Tone 4	"0"	ling4	ling
Tone 5	"5"	ng5	mm
Tone 6	"2"	ji6	yee

ALTERNATE PRONUNCIATIONS

For words with more than one common pronunciation, this book tries to select the pronunciation that would be most easily understood when spoken by less fluent Cantonese speakers. For example, for 你(you): both "lei5 (lay)" and "nei5 (nay)" are common pronunciations. This book uses "nei (nay)", since less fluent Cantonese speakers may find they are more easily understood.

ABOUT THE AUTHOR

Karen Yee graduated from Stanford University and the Wharton School of Business, and was a National Spelling Bee finalist. She was inspired to create Cantonese bilingual books and the Cantonese for Kids series to help her own family have fun learning languages.